ROMANTIC COMEDY

FOUR WAY BOOKS
TRIBECA

POEMS

ROMANTIC COMEDY

JAMES ALLEN HALL

Library of Congress Cataloging-in-Publication Data

Names: Hall, James Allen, 1976– author.
Title: Romantic comedy / James Allen Hall.
Description: New York : Four Way Books, [2023]
Identifiers: LCCN 2022033085 (print) | LCCN 2022033086 (ebook)
| ISBN 9781954245464 (paperback) | ISBN 9781954245471 (epub)
Subjects: LCGFT: Poetry.
Classification: LCC PS3608.A54725 R66 2023 (print) | LCC PS3608.A54725
(ebook) | DDC 811/.6—dc23/eng/20220715
LC record available at https://lccn.loc.gov/2022033085
LC ebook record available at https://lccn.loc.gov/2022033086

This book is manufactured in the United States of America
and printed on acid-free paper.

Funding for this book was provided
in part by a generous donation
in memory of John J. Wilson.
This publication is made possible with public funds
from the New York State Council on the Arts, a state agency.

We are a proud member of the Community of Literary Magazines and Presses.

CONTENTS

Notes

for my friends, who told me stories

Comedy is tragedy plus time.
—Carol Burnett

Biography

I was made for.
Made in. Made to.
I was dolled, posed
for every eye. Was
made for drama
I confess I lied. I
was manmade in
an Indiana factory,
the first factor
my parents agreed.
Was a handmade
doll brought out
to sing for company.
Pull my string, I
laughed. Too high,
a little long. My
pitch was wrong.
Wooden. Was a hand
made lap, sewn up
dummy. Wore the story
I was made for. Told
the truths. Cold
wind whistled in
the hollows. I sang
the terrible songs
while undressed.
Who else was made

to entertain you.
Was one done up.
Done for. Bullseyed,
buried. This story
is mine: there was
a wound, then a world.
It did not mean
me well. One year
I watched the snow
pile to my door
all December, all
January. This was
the year I wanted
to die. Learned
another song. Sang
another way.

I.

Joke ISO Punch Line

I only heard one joke the month I spent in Zürich.
I was in bed with a wry-eyed economist
who was saying, *When the urge thickens in me*
like a wet and heavy snow, I want to find a field
and shoot myself. His neckless head was propped
on one arm, he laughed at my jaw dropped
open, my eyebrows furrowed—the face of pity.
I didn't say it was a funny joke. I didn't say anything.

I contemplated leaving, flinging myself out
the door in my camo jacket. But I stayed. I stayed
because I lied about where I was from,
because it was my hotel, and our heads were citizens
of the same pillow. In his eyes, snow was beginning
to cover the field. I couldn't leave him in a blizzard

so I told him about the time I drove into a swarm
of butterflies, auburn monarchs blotting out
the Swiss countryside. I rolled up the windows,
turned off the air, but the bodies slipped in
through the vents, slicking my arms, my face.

My hero, he allowed. Then he was kicking out of bed,
shifting into charcoal-colored slacks. I touched his back,
touched him to keep him, to forget the fact that this all
happens here, now, in America, in my bed,

where we are untangling ourselves from sheets
I haven't washed in a month of Sundays—since
my boyfriend left the house I inhabit like a runaway
divorcée, where I wish for all the wings in the world
I wasn't living. *Butterfly blood is clear and viscous,*

it can't stain you, I say over the hum of his Jeep,
in the carport, through the window he rolls down
to slip a scrawled name and number. *I would love,*
he says, *to see your face again, commandeered
by broken orange wing.* His smile is tight, crooked,
like italics on crumpled paper.

When I call, the recorded voice advises, *hang up,*
try again. What else should I do but laugh,
my face buried in my own two living hands?

Lie Down Where Their Faces Are

My neighbor shuts his wife outside again. *Love ritual,*
my therapist calls it: the wife pleads, the husband lets her
suffer until the right degree of *sorry* shivers into her voice.
I hate him—the best mechanic in the town's only garage—
because he once interrogated me in his shop until
I admitted, *I may not know front from rear-wheel drive,*
but I can name the three types of sonnets, and he laughed,
saying I should drive a poem then. I wish I could
stop her climbing those three concrete steps
after the door's unlocked. But a body wants a darkness
it doesn't face alone. Sometimes I picture my therapist
watching naked as I count the pills, piling them into white
pyramids, my unflinching confessors. No body should be
this cold or up this late. Even the neighbors' mutt is asleep,
tree-chained, head between his paws, dream-running past
the cars rusting out on the lawn. One night, ritual concluded,
the dog breaks free into the forest, his black fur a blur
against trees that recede into a depth so impenetrable it is sacred.
The next morning the man knocks. I make him wait.
"Have ya seen m'dog?" he asks, fists stuffed in jacket pockets.
He is a man who needs to imagine himself some thing's lord
and savior. A body wants a purpose. Otherwise,
it's only a thwarted engine waiting shockeyed
for repair. The dog will become a fable about real and invisible
chains, what happens when brute and devotee share a plot.

Lie down. It's late. Time to sleep, orders the god of enumerating pills.
I lie down but can't stop the voice turning over and over,
igniting in me: *fled, the animal will live forever.*

Mise~en~Scène

Driving to see you, I try to guess the houses
where women are chained in blank rooms.

The oranges in the grocery store on your street
slump jawless in their display crate.

In the closet, your shirt dangles on its hanger
by the neck.

A bedroom open to winter light
is darker than any unlit room.

The geese splatter up from the ground,
into a red sky.

You undress me gently. I close my eyes
and try to imagine anything

but the corn stalks slid like knives
into their hardened block of field.

Swimming Lesson

Keep your legs together! Your body is a knife!
I heave myself through the water,
towards the tiles forming a black cross
at the far end, where I flip my body,
propel it into the past, into the wake
of its own trek. Two weeks, and he hasn't
hurt me yet, my swim coach lover, yelling
down into the water. I can't love
an incapable man. My body is a knife.

*

Our swimsuits drip-drying on the towel rack at home,
and I have just made him come

when he rolls away and says, *I can't. Your body*
repulses me, your fat.... There are more words after

but I let them drown. For another month,
he fucks his repulsion into me.

Harm given tenderly, purposefully—
I have learned to thirst for it.

Putting the I Back In

I love the I / for its premise of existence—
—"Take the I Out," Sharon Olds

.

The most exorbitant thing is a man, kicked.
You've come to pathetic his neck.
You're standing above his kneeling body.
The coal-filth of Pittsburgh dominates
the hotel window, its eye propped open
with a piece of wood, made to watch.
Choke the dog collar tighter until he submits
his entire mud-puddled-Liberty-Avenue-
customer-service-9-to-5 life. Gutter his breath.
Pat the head. Jab open the square jaw.
Order his tongue out and strike the match
until it lights. Feeble his teeth. Say bite,
say bitch, he'll clench the flaming stick
as you start a votive candle. The hot wax
cooling before his face can even flinch.
This is how you teach a language:
sound before sense. I must have no sense.
I must be tongueless. If I were here
in this poem, I wouldn't stay to witness
voluntary pain, men making love
in a language marked by slur and Sir.
But I'm not writing this. I'm in the room
with you, a scald coating my cheek.
Kneel down, make our faces meet.
Kiss this thing you've made of fire.

Night Watch

after Allen Ginsberg

Please Master, it's winter, warm yourself
with my mouth. A man loved me,

then he didn't. Please, don't let me be
mastered by another. Master,

the stung-cold trees seduce no one
but me. Please, Master, make me myopic,

make me ruin myself for a match.
In the city's cast-off light, I'll never be masculine,

normal. The light could mean *inferno*;
the sound of cars, *hold me fast*; please,

Master, your stubble burns my tongue,
I'll never sound the same. Please, Master,

deprive me of firewood, leave me
depraved, extinguish the need in me to please.

Master, my doors are broken, wood splintered
as marriage. Master, the tree branches, brittle

with ice. Everywhere I turn I see frailty.
My bones are alone in my body. Master

my body, I'll be your collared night.
Your burned-out moon. I'll show you

what endures will smolder in the snow,
healing itself. Smotemouthed, smitten.

A fireplace, all smoke. But you made
the mouth too, Lord, for yours, Lord,

this mouth to hold you safe,
my mouth now palled past pleading.

Erotic Crime Thriller

Cruising (1980)

It's just a flimsy mattress
in a hookup motel, a night
when the moon is a single stud
in a leather sky. Just a bed
smelling of spilled poppers,
until two men enter.
Then it's a story: one lays
himself naked, face-down,
offering his wrists, ankles
to be rope-knotted, the thrill
of seeing what exists after
extremity. The movie's first
image: a hand floating
in a helpless river, cross-fading
into a couple of male cops
forcing two queer sex
workers, their painted mouths.
All sex is a body trying
to tell a story with a hand
over its mouth. Because this
is erotic crime, what follows
are hours of leather bar dancing,
the ball-sweat skulking
off the celluloid, and plenty
of interrogation. The killer
spreads like a plague—

first one nondescript actor
plays him, then another,
until the undercover cop
catches the serial virus, this
being 1980, the end of innocent
beds, of innocuous jocks,
foam parties, condomless
trade. As if the director—
in conjuring the end of taboo
in strobe light, in dim urinals,
in park bushes, under the
spinning doom of moon—
in trying to make us subject
has subjected us to ravage instead.
My friend says I'm dramatic,
says you can't blame art
for epidemiology. Forgive me.
I have come here to the river,
to the bed, to the foaming edge
of time, to 1980, a year before
the first reported cases. I have
come with my one good hand
and all my blood and I will say
anything to save us.

The Saw

Museo de la Tortura, Toledo, Spain

Someone heated the iron, cut one side jagged. A man
          hoisted the criminal up. Angled
the saw at his scrotum. *Criminal*, because he followed
          a plainclothes soldier home,
kissed him open-eyed, saw night shredded down
          to morning, saw too late
in his lover's closet the uniforms, legs halved by hanging.
          The prayer to bless the saw
is beautiful. *Sierra*: my lover corrects my tongue
          as we stand in the museum,
our hands pressed against the stained glass of the wrong
          century. Steel pig masks stare back
beside the wrack, the maiden, the ghostly pontiff hoods,
          eyeing my wrists. Last night I was
suspect, he the guard tying me down, turning me from witness
          into tool, body hammered into new
use. How easily its pliancy the flesh forgets. It took me hours
          before I could re-enter myself.
The sharpness perforating me. Today I am following the man
          as if he is my home. I let him
shut me inside the iron maiden because I want to know
          the interior history of pain,
to love the force in the world that wants me torn apart.

The Villain

1.
I couldn't bear to wash the sheets, replace
Brandon's scent with "mountain breeze."

The first man I saw after the breakup:
used car salesman who, post-coitus,

cleaned himself with his Megadeath concert tee.
He saw a photo of my ex and said,

"You let a n——— put his cock in you?"
I threw him out, wouldn't take his calls,

so he told his friends I sucked him off
while he watched his favorite Western.

Now, every gay bar Pittsburgh yinzer
calls me *Desperado.*

2.
One bad boy gave me good coke;
one bad boy wrote for a reality TV show
but wouldn't scrub his own toilet.

Bad boy friend of bad boy barkeep:
I can see you have a type. I paid for the taxi
back to my place. He didn't stay the night.

Tall bad boy grinning down at me:
What a great fat ass you have. Bad
boy Aries, bad boy Virgo, two Geminis

and a slew of Scorpios whose mothers
gave me pep talks at Sunday brunch.
Bad boy who gave me chrysanthemums

and chlamydia. Bad boy whose résumé
I fluffed. Bad boy who got sober:
Our spiritual journeys just don't mesh.

3.
Brandon announced he was leaving
because his mother had cancer, and I felt
relieved: now neither of us had to be the villain.
Tonight I let a man snake himself across my body
after sex. When he started to snore, I let myself
out, drove home counting the trees I didn't hit,
the splinterless minutes of my life. I plotted
how best to punish myself for turning out like this.

4.
One gave me roses each time we met
at the theater, red embarrassment
he insisted I carry so my hands would hold
something besides that buttered tub of popcorn.

One threw away the bouquet I sent
him at work, said I was *marking* him.

One gave me marguerites to celebrate
our one-week anniversary, *one for every day*.
I told him I was seeing other people;
I wasn't.

The one I remember easiest gave me aloe,
cutting it to rub on the small burns I got
cooking him dinner.

The one I remember worst gave me jasmine,
night-blooming, potted tangle, tight-budded green.
I remember his instructions: shut it away
in a dark dry room for a week, then shock it
with water and sunlight. It will bloom, he said,

out of sheer gladness.

5.
If half of love is feeling   endangered.
If a villain isn't   born.
If a man is   broken.
If he wants to   break something
back. If there is an   equal
and an opposite. If no   story

can exist without   a threat.
If we take turns. If we   need
to take turns. If I   cannot abandon
him. If he cannot   let go of me.
If our dread and dolor   lodge
in other bodies   instead.
If we turn away.   If we return.
If the end too   is a violence
we cannot visit   upon each other.
If the end is never allowed. If we refuse
to be cruel   once,
are we cruel   forever?

Stock Character

Jumped from a bridge,
from the top of a
tenement, from the
window; jumped in
front of a train, in
front of a bus; jumped
into a noose, hanging
from the barn rafter,
in the room's dim
closet, noose from the
doorjamb, from an elm
in a thicket seen aerially
from afar, thicket from
which, after a gunshot,
crows fly up, a metaphor
for the queer boy we
can't see falling.

The Bridge

Prologue
In the novel I love, the main character
leaps off the George Washington Bridge
—eighty pages in, the architecture fails.
A bloated face surfaces every time
his surviving friends embrace.

1.
Let the bridge stand for chronology.
I am in a man's apartment, looking out
at the bridge from his picture window,
our first time meeting, his pianist fingers
playing up the suspension wires
of my spine, then taking my suitcase.
If only the bridge would collapse,
I could see how I'm rescued.

2.
At Rufus's funeral, Vivaldo is still interpreting the dream:
he and Rufus wrestling in a bed in their underwear,

Rufus's grip on his neck tightening, Vivaldo can't breathe.
He failed his best friend, he thinks the dream convicts him.

He doesn't know the dream isn't two men: it's just him,
broken into two desires. I don't pity him.

I pity the story which is either about desire or destruction,
or about how they are just different abutments

of the same bridge. I pity the story, arching concrete
over the diminishing world. Or maybe I do pity Vivaldo.

He thinks meaning is always available, the inevitable
bridging desire from the symbolic to the explicable.

Meanwhile, the river washes in
on itself, bearing the dead man home.

3.
When the man lowered his body to mine,
I bit his shoulder, I divided him too.

I won't suffer time's deliberate amputation.
I won't live without retaliating.

4.
I took off my clothes for him.
Then I was on my back.

It was not without sweetness.
Violence wants someone to receive it,

give it form, hold it, hum to it,
brush the hair away from its forehead.

Epilogue
Sleep tunes him to innocent again.
I open the window, no screen.

I light my cigarette, the bridge
in the distance almost glowing

from within its bracing,
arcing through summer fog.

The sky in New York,
it won't give up. The red sirens

going blue beneath me,
redoubling the island.

From here, I must look
penitent, believing

if I close my eyes,
this can all be stopped.

One Train's Survival
Depends on the Other Derailed

after Susan Mitchell

In a bar in Chicago like a bar in New York, the anthems hang
in jukebox air: *I Will Survive, Maybe This Time, Don't Leave Me*

This Way, the bartender's nipple ring catching the disco ball's
shrapnel light on a night which begins in wan November, dancing

with a chestnut-haired Aries, the scorch of us hurtling like a train
I want to step in front of. He takes my hand when we leave the bar,

walking a greasy sidewalk to a private courtyard. He kisses me
under a magnolia as fragrant as the one in the garden where I hid

as a boy, the tree's opalescent sepals masking my upturned face.
I'd fall asleep there, playing soldier, dreaming of a real-life G.I. Joe

come to the rescue, smiling down into the plot, shovel in hand.
He kisses me on a night so rinsed in purity it begs for its
    own ending.

The night's begging lodged in me. We're parallel trains lurching
forward, jaunting windows jaggedly aligned. Don't love the train,

it craves to be emptied. When we part, a February
   starfield blooming
in the dead of winter: *Don't miss me,* he says, at the stairs to
   the F train,

saying goodbye with a sterile hug. I miss the stars, which leaned
   in close.
In November, I could die happy, his saliva drying on my neck,

the breeze violining along the sloped avenue. The song expires
in an overheated car speeding eastward into the night, the snow

lowering its gentle hammer on the skulls of lovers, the night
   I know
in my sudden blood I am going to kill myself. Don't miss me,

the disco-ball moon says to the lake. Don't miss me says a boy
to the plastic partition, the snow melting down his face in tracks,

in February, on a night stricken at last of starlight, shocked dumb,
night with its shovel and its covering dark.

Genre Theory

I could be chain-watching *The Real Housewives of New Jersey*
when fantasy breaks in, usurping commercial interlude:

I could be in a field, gun entering my mouth, roughing my teeth.
I am powerless against the wind swelling,

echoing through the abandoned church in an empty field.
I watch my body fall. How peace rules all the land then.

*

How do you say, *Once upon a time there was a limitless sky*
above a golden field where I pull a trigger. Once upon a time
could mean *in media res* or the archaic past's every day.
Do I begin, *Once upon a time I fell in love with ending?*
Is it a love story when the desire is unspeakable?

*

In our story, what tense is the narrator utilizing?
Call it *historical present,* time tinted, tipped toward urgency.

What tense best fits a hero who falls out of time,
turning into a tree whose branches end in axeblades?

*

Voice like wind winding between the sharpness.
Voice like a mourning dove leaving its nest
and one day it doesn't return. Who can say why.
The science is lost to us.

A Home in the Country

In unpaved Kennedyville, not far from the Bight,
on five acres of green organic farm,
next to the algaed pond that yields the best fishing
in Kent County (my neighbor says it is
a *lingering* death I deal the trout
when he sees me throw the small ones back),
down where the commonest cars are tractors
and hayfetchers, and men wave as they pass, briefly
bowing a gentleman's straw hat, you can find
the wood cabin infested with stink bugs, where I live.
Every day, my boyfriend asks the *murder count*,
making light of my hatred. Even reading
I sit with a swatter poised on the couch's arm,
all the windows closed, fans off, the whole house
listening for the *thwack* of stink on sun-warmed glass,
their soft-backed geometric carapaces calling
to be stopped. I did not grow up like this, here
on Maryland's Eastern Shore, but I am most at home
now I live with something inside to kill.

Monument

Boldt Castle, Heart Island, Alexandria, NY

It is a place untouched by irony.
The visitor's parlor darkens our faces
as the welcome-film begins: violins
sweeping us across Heart Island,
through heavy heart-shaped doors
into the empty miniature Rhineland Castle.
What's more real—the film or the fact
that I'm sitting too close to every straight
summer-vacationing couple in upstate
New York, feeling like an accomplice
to building a mini-shrine to their kind
of marriage? The narrator: *George Boldt*
ordered the island trimmed to resemble a heart
—a present for his wife, Louise, born February 14.

Cue the montage: George and Louise strolling
the frozen river, mink coats raking snow;
George and Louise waltzing in the ballroom;
George and Louise posing in the hennery,
falcons perched on upraised arms. Always
George to camera, Louise quarter-turned,
blurred, evading capture. *Tragedy soon cut in*
—Louise heart-attacked at 41, *and George abandons*
Heart Island forever. The final shot iris-outs

into a heart. When the lights come up
on the Island of Straight Amorists, half
are crying, the other half blinking hard,
trying to see the happy ending they expected.
I'd be lying if I said I wasn't satisfied
by their tears. It's better to live in the clock tower,
on the river's edge—anywhere but inside
this fairy tale where every monument becomes

a mausoleum. The castle stands unfinished:
docents encourage you to leave your name
on the plaster which is every autumn erased
anew. If I was only built to leave you,
love, I would not leave you here.

II.

Prophecy

Remember, my mother says, *they found Adam Walsh
in pieces*, buttoning my jacket, kissing my cheek,
sending me off to school, directly across
the dead-end road. Street severed by woods,
I couldn't shake its prophecy. In school, we play
Hangman: on the chalkboard, a neck in a rope,
a word underneath in dashes, letters looming
from the fog, filling in the blanks, until
one grinning boy hangs another.

Image

Catherine Opie, *Self-Portrait/Cutting*.
Chromogenic print, 40 inches x 29 inches (1993).
Guggenheim Museum, NYC.

The artist-model turns away from us,
her hair shorn to the nape,

a barb-wire tattoo circling her tricep,
which, when flexed, is a warrior's,

but for now hangs limp as any
unpoisoned spear. She is naked,

an image seared on her back:
a house, two windows, a door.

Two open eyes and a shut mouth.
All the poisoned words are in bed,

looking out to the garden:
two girls in red skirts hold hands

among the tulips. The artist can't see
them smiling. I tell her she can

drop the knife, but there's a bruise
the size of a fist at the base

of her neck. She won't stop drawing
the same girls, the same garden,

in her blood, on her body.
The house could be a school,

the drawing a lesson: the scar
of your childhood will never heal.

Harlequin

My mother is making love to a policeman
in a church parking lot. The illuminated cross
shines through the metal partition, mirrorballing
her naked back. Her spine arches, the squad
car buckles on gravel. The radio sounds
its static serenade. My mother can't hear
my father approach from the line of slash pines,
can't know how afraid he is to see her,
how he suddenly wishes he wasn't wearing khakis,
his paisley tie embarrassed by soup at lunch.
He has to see her so he can stop it,
the other man's hand stroking his wife's
honey-blonde hair. But he can't take another step.
My father takes the gun from his waistband,
cleans it, both sides, on his slacks.

*

Sometimes at night I hear them arguing
behind their door. I can't sleep. I read
my mother's Harlequins in the laundry,
my head propped on a pile of unwashed dresses.
In my favorite fantasy, I'm the captured nurse,
refusing to surrender to the foreign sergeant,
who's fighting to liberate the fortress of her desire.
Both of them looking at each other like a wound,

judging its fatality. It's so quiet I can hear
the moment the crying clicks off. Then I patrol,
hands clasped, index fingers jutting, my pantomime
gun. I am a robbery in progress, prowling
Charlie's Angel with 70s bangs. I aim
at the dirty dishes, chipped faces half-submerged
in the sink, I aim at my brothers, asleep
in their beds. I aim for a punishing kind of love.
Like my father, unable to fire or forgive.

Bypass

The sky is an overcast bruise all winter in Indiana,
where I was born. My father sits in his wheelchair
and asks, *Why didn't you let me die?* repeating it
for my brother when he enters the room.
We didn't think he'd come back from the stroke,
the coma, the quadruple bypass. We didn't know
he'd come back cur-tongued, racist, refusing
to eat, frightening in his hospital bed at home,
sheets sharpened by piss. In the days before
the hospital, we were his caretakers. *Don't call
the ambulance,* he begged. *Ok, dad,* I'd said,
until one day I motioned for Dustin to call
as I massaged our father's shoulders, encouraging
his blood. His heart was blocked. My mother was gone.

Once, my father told me he loved me. I was eight.
I hated him for the nights my mother left the house
in red silk, trailing spice. *You're my son*, he said.
His hug insisted harder. My forehead right-angled
against his chest, blacking out the blue Florida sky.
I hung my arms straight at my sides. I didn't know
the story you try hardest to avoid passes into you,
forms an interior weather, arranges your veins.

Boyhood

In the famous painting, God's touch becomes Adam.
Or He *nearly* touches, proving desire, not God, is the father

of man. Still the question: What does He want with Adam's body?
To take it back, take Adam into His arms?

Maybe God too feels regret and longing?
God-like is God-damned. No father can be trusted.

This Adam too surrendered in a wilderness,
the snake cleaving the thick silver grasses.

Adam names the grass, uses it to thatch a makeshift roof.
The word he used doesn't survive.

The grass also was born without enmity.
Adam is an experiment, a hypothesis without boyhood.

How many prototypes blighted the field?

Blackberries

Grandma marches us barefoot at dusk into brambles.
My feet are calloused, but he's ten, my little brother,
and when he gets thorned, begins to cry, I turn us
houseward, carrying his weight. *Someone ought to toughen
you up,* I hear Grandma mutter. *Goddamn you* spits
like a seed between my lips before I can reckon right.
The dusk holds its breath, the blackberries stiffen
their spines. Suddenly I know what I am capable of,
and for whom. I am sent to my room without dinner,
am summerlong exiled, forced to pick the blackberries
—and lychees, too, reaching from ladders affixed
to white vans, my brother calling up, high climbing
notes, his voice yet to drop, *Someone ought to....*
And I call down, *Goddamn you,* then we're taking turns,
reversing the parts, relishing the tart sting on our tongues.

Genre Theory

"Happiness," George Burns says, "is having
a large, loving, caring, close-knit family
in another city." Houston hosted
the Republican National Convention in '92,
when we lived in Florida, a safe distance away
from Pat Robertson telling the country
that Clinton wanted "to repeal the ban
on homosexuals," part of his "radical plan
to destroy the traditional family." At least
one pope called the family unit "the first
essential cell of human society." HIV
was first named Gay-Related Immune
Deficiency in May of '82. Family: a cell
that duplicates, unthinkingly. When I chose
for Movie Night, I was notorious
for selecting stories about people like me:
Peter's Friends or *Philadelphia, Being
at Home with Claude, The Hanging Garden.*
My family protested I had a radical plan
to make myself visible. Nevermind that
the gay men always died. I should have
picked Haynes and Almodóvar, Van Sant
and Araki. I didn't know then how to elect
my own family. Derived from Latin, *famulitas,*
meaning servitude. As when my uncle
kissed my sister on the stairs and she confessed

to me, then hissed, *Writing this will mean*
betrayal. Family: why do I hear *failingly?*
Family: something you leave
if you want to stay alive.

At Home with Adam Walsh

Adam is afraid of the dark, we sleep with the TV on silent.
He climbs down from his bunk, lays on top of me
in our superhero underwear. *Let's wrestle,* he says,
I get to be Rick Rude. He teaches me first The Sleeper,
then Hangman's Choke, twisting my arm up
to show where the ligature marks will, he says,
make clean crosses with your veins. I rub my wrists
and tell him I want to stop playing Tie Me Up.
He never wants to be saved anymore.
Fine, then help me teach your brother.

Poppies in October

Interstate 70 is a charred artery through Ohio
until we reach Columbus and its Ten Commandments
billboards: italics singed red against black,
lit up at night. Brimstone, sobering scripture.
Thou shalt not covet thy neighbour's ox, nor his ass,
our first laugh in two hundred miles.
Two states away, our grandmother is dying.
My brother is driving because he is good
at passing the truckers, good at spotting cops
concealed in cornfields. I should know by now,
but I'm ignorant as a husk. You can't see through a dark
you haven't lived. Can't understand the poppy
unless you've been a seedhead in an unfastening wind,
can't understand the wind unless you've entered a room
blued by smoke, two men in their underwear
crushing crystals saying, *It isn't for you, pretty boy,*
so you wait for them to leave, then lay fire to the pipe's bed,
my brother's first time high, becoming a man
trying to unhear the gospel ugly. Even this poem can't help
becoming a billboard I want to whitewash.
But it's the truth. And it is a sin to say it here,
where just anyone can read it. My brother tries so hard
to keep between the lines, intent, fixed on piercing
through the coal-shimmering dark to whatever lies beyond.

My Grandmother Slams Crystal Meth
the First Time, Four Months after Her Death

My brother is kissing a man who's brought a Ziploc
of crystal and two rubber bands. On the television, gay porn.

But my grandmother hasn't finished dying yet, not where
the meth descends. And now my brother's hands are hers,

feeling for the curlers, arthritic through her permed hair.
The lucent part of him remembering the blackberrying,

the dinner theater musicals, the vapor rub, her perennial scent.
Instead of gay porn, what my grandmother is watching

are black and white home movies, made the year
Mother Wilde died, oh how your grandfather hated her

but he let me keep her Tiffany lamp. I liked how the colors
turned in the brief chandelier. The man beside my brother blinks,

almost remembering too, almost again someone's grandson.
There you are in my bedroom, my little Zsa Zsa, trying on dresses.

You got your coal eyes from my side, but that mess you're in now
from your mother's. She pinches his elbow and laughs.

The man shakes his head. *Shut the fuck up,* he says
to my brother who sniffs, clutching for invisible pearls.

Young man, he chides, his voice breaking,
that is no way to talk to your grandmother.

Pittsburgh

I burn your Highland Park. I acid your Carnegie
car dealerships. Your Squirrel Hill, sheer terror
in winter. But most of all, I hate your Liberty Avenue,
the last place, one night, I saw my little brother
saying, *Wait here*, outside the after-hours club
as he disappears around the corner. I wait,
hating your Strip, half your Shadyside, all of Bloomfield,
the bluffs and flats where he trades himself.
I wait hours, then trace your Mexican War
Streets looking for my brother's car, so I could declare
a truce in the battle he was fighting against himself.
Your Hot Metal, your Fort Pitt Bridge that leads
headfirst into the Monongahela. In the morning,
he's home. He cannot tell me where it hurts.
I help him shower off the Duquesne residue,
the priesting old-world shame. Pittsburgh,
you're all grit and gristle turning crystal
track marks, a man meth-mouth.
I feed him, put him to bed. I'll keep watch tonight
in a cable car ascending Mt. Washington,
your smokestacks blowing clouds over the confluence
until all you are, Pittsburgh, is a sleepless shimmer
I will watch diminish down to the savaged seed
of morning, as impossible to watch
as you are to name.

Adam Walsh, in Pieces

Mother always said, *But you have such a beautiful face.*
Said, *You can't be hungry again already.*

After my older brother told her I'd been raped,
my mother said, *That explains a lot about you.*

From where he sits in the backyard tree house
in my mind, Adam smirks. A good boy

likes to be held down. The next boyfriend
says, *Did you fight? Did some part of you*

want it to happen? Adam stands quiet in the garden.
He has no mother. *Do you want it to happen again?*

Love, a kind of kidnap. A good boy would slap
a man's hand away. Instinct. Manners.

The next boyfriend says:
Didn't your mother teach you how?

Wisdom

Curse the wisdom saying I must
learn to turn my back again
on my little brother.

Bless the dealer's squat prefab house,
the blackout curtains that keep out
the glaring afternoon. Bless the roaches,

numbed now to their filters in the quartz
ashtray, smudging gray across the sleeper's
face when the air conditioner tumbles on,

smoke-sour as his breath. Keep out
the bad dreams, keep the elastic off his bicep,
the needle away from his sating vein.

Praise the floor on which he lies,
my brother bent like a burnt spoon,
hands curled up to his chest, hands

stayed against turning himself to ash
for now. He used to sleep that way
in the bedroom we shared as kids,

on the floor, in a house like this,
curtains drawn, lawn untended,
a person inside trying to die. We slept

back-to-back on the thin carpet,
under the same blanket, under the static
playing softly from the portable radio,

drowning out the terminal sadness
of that house. Bless the floor
that holds him now I cannot.

At the Table

Thanksgiving, and someone etched the word *bitch*
into my grandmother's car. She tells the story
at the table, blushing red as her rusted Ford.
My older brother, shirtless, stabs his food
with a bowie knife, licks it clean, still a boy
at 27, passing her a criminal's smile.
She ignores him, occupied as she is with jagged
letters made by jealous geriatric girlfriends—
at eighty-two, she's the other woman, too proud
to have it fixed, driving Miami half-blind
in a cussword car, improved by scandal.
This is our family pastime, disguising shame
in story; we sharpen our tongues with our knives.

When it comes to pass that my grandmother can tell
no more stories, my brother comes alone,
past visiting hours, past ineffectual, objecting nurses
who tell me later how he sat for an hour,
telling her body his grief: times she made him ask
rather than offer the money, saying, *Go to work,*
saying, *You have to watch him,* every gripe a version
of the same story: you looked at me
with the word *adopted* scratched across your eyes.

He tells her it was he who booby-trapped
the greenhouse all those years ago;
now it does not matter, he can say she deserved it.

I picture them in the dark together, and I
cannot see which I have sharpened out to be:
woman lying mute as a table, or the man etched through.

My Father Calls to Say the Walls Are on Fire

By which he means nothing as extraordinary as sunrise
coming in through his window, and I say, *Dad,*
what time is it there, because he can still read digital hours,
and he says, *You're on fire, all of us smoke, look out your window.*

There's only the magnolia arming itself against Houston,
oil refineries pluming smoke into the air, and my neighbor
starting her gray Impala, driver-side door open, one leg
dangling outside as she reverses, her full skirt brushing
lilac against the ground. I've never lived anywhere
so insistent on pastel, on hair tailored into a tulip's bloom.
I don't see anything, Dad, I say, sighing, turning on the television

to hear the air purity report. *It's only dark in your eyes,* he says,
which is what he'd always say when I was a kid begging him
to switch on the light after his ghost story, and he'd laugh,
saying the light was already on, and how many times
did I believe him, rubbing my eyes until stars appeared?

But now I can't get to him, lead him back to bed, saying,
I made it all up, I'm sorry, I made up that whole story.
It's 8 in the morning, it's too early for this. Please stop
being sick. My father insists, *danger* but I'm not listening.
The television is on and some god made a fist

and punched through the World Trade Center, ordered the city
below to run, not all of us will survive. Without

knowing I'm talking at all, I'm saying, *No, Dad*, repeating it,
because a god made me too, and sometimes denial
is my only religion: he isn't getting worse, my father
isn't deranged, pissing on the neighbor's lawn.
He's still a citizen, the man who told tall tales, preparing me

for this world hazed in smoke, where the tower was always
made of a burnt falling, the brain always a matter of surrender.
Memory demolishes; it wants things whole: my father
still telling stories, a flashlight under his chin, his face reddened,
eyes like caves, his hair already receding.

Gift

Dora's coming, Larry, let's get some pants on,
the home-nurse says to lure my father
into civilized behavior. Forty years since
he saw the girl he was baptized Mormon for,
since he sat beside her in his first serious car,
parked at high tide on Daytona Beach,
desire taking them past the white lifejackets,
shedding clothes, naked into the tide,
bodies flashing like Polaroids in the dark
Atlantic. When my father tries to remember,
he raises his good hand as if he might draw her
out of the Lethe, but memory has sewn shut,
made a mannequin of the girl he lost
his virginity to. A month ago, I found
his leftover Cialis, one blue pill rattling
in its plastic orange ossuary, and under his bed,
a Mason jar of moonshine, all formaldehyde
and no brain. I swallowed the pill
with the booze, to feel what he wanted
to save. For Dora, he allowed his hair washed,
combed, his face freshly shaven—no struggle,
no punches if the nurse caught a tangle.
My resuscitated father, sitting up straight
in his wheelchair, practicing his posture.
Stroke-stricken, heart-attacked, hip-replaced,
my toothless father, trying not to soil
his diaper, delivered back from the erasing foam.

On Dark Days, I Imagine
My Parents' Wedding Video

My mother, Anita Bryant, waves to the cameras
without looking at the men behind them, her chastity
intact, unassailable as her perfect coiffure, dark
as coffee, the white saucer of her face. The news
conference is a whirl of men, microphones. *Save*
the Children blaring on a banner behind her.
I am waiting to be born, a child unlike others,
one my mother would not save. The reporters'
blazers are plaid, unbuttoned; he's disguised
like them, the man approaching the dais,
my father. I love my mother, innocent, smiling
at the softball questions, I like the hiding in plain
sight that the man and the Anita are doing
before they become my parents. I like knowing
more than the camera. And here is the moment,
their kiss: the man slaps a pie square in Anita's face.
She hadn't seen him coming. She was saying,
What they want is the right to propose to our children
that theirs is an acceptable life. Then it's time for cake.
I like his hate which hates her back. She is my mother
because she says, *At least it's a fruit pie,* then begins
to sob. I like watching her dissolve,
thirty years ago now, my father dead, buried,
and no one remembers his name.

III.

Post-Apocalyptic Horror Show
Ending in a Cher Song

The AIDS metaphor: what we imagine best,
virus buried in every zombie movie,
turning its host to living death.

My bemused boyfriend argues that zombies
don't have sex, are ahistorical, just nostalgia
cut down to the guttural, the final image

in this queer apocalypse. Of course the zombies
outlive the heteros. They herd in and out
of the all-American diner, lurching

their suited bodies against the jukebox,
Cher's disembodied voice pressing free:
"I Found Someone," her brassy tenor

trumpeting over the broken dishes,
the open stinking freezers, thawed steaks
sloughed out like forgotten skins.

The threat is always someone else's fear.
Imagine—what the world wanted all along:
a song, a way to remember us.

Stock Character

Man with Gun at His Temple. Man with Pills.
Man Hanged, Man Stabbed, Man Crushed

by Oncoming Tractor-Trailer. Man Throbbing
with Death Wish, Man with One Leg

Already Over the Precipice. It's like
I invented him in a romantic comedy

so stale it needs a body count to liven
things up. It's like he jumps

from one story to another, trying to find
the one where he gets to live. But I can't

just waltz in and tell Man with Razor
at Wrist he's a trope. Man, Terminal

with American Imagination Deteriorating Syndrome
is never out of work. Just last week

on *Law and Disorder*, he suicided unironically
in a posh Miami salon. I could contradict

every role, but my body looks good
half-caged in straight imagination.

Irregular Plurals

A pile of sticks bound for the pyre—
it's easy to forget *faggot* is already plural.

Every plural scissors its singular,

everything pieces back to one,
the problem of oranges and orchard,
the problem a cut apple spits out to its seeds.

Example: the plural of story is history.

I is ad infinitum. The plural of thinking
is feeling. My problem is the article I
read yesterday about the window and the boy.
I'll come back for them. I'm sorry

I can't stop a thing from accumulating.

Add an –s, an –es. Archaic, how we think
adding more makes a story bearable.
The plural of broken is suicide. The plural
of string is harps, just as the plural
of hand is jobs. Shiver of. Quiver in.

There is no one pleasure when words fail.

This is true of pain as well, and that is
the plural of epiphany. It feels monstrous
to be saved more than once, so the plural
of we must be Jesus. The plural of once
I was raped is every day after.
The plural victim growing inside me, garden

proliferating past its seed. Think

of the sixteen-year-old boy, jumping
from the building's fourth-story window,
limbs seeking singularity the moment
the john unties the restraints that keep him
the plural of bed. Cruelty is its own plural.
It makes me glad to say he survived,
that boy is somewhere breathing, making

my lives shudder into focus.

Hart Crane Aboard the Steamship *Orizaba*

The waves slip under each other, one story drowns another.

I fell in love last night with a member of the crew;
he beat me the moment we were alone in my cabin.

This is the bridge I have to cross out. The dark makes the cold
colder inside me.

This steamship's white railing, the boundary of sense.
There is a line I must cross.

If my father needs to, he can say, *My son carried the night within him.*

I cross these distances with my voice. Lean close now.
Pin every romantic ending on my shirt, wet from sea-spray.

But keep me dry in your story, put me on a little island
riddled with orange trees, with a mangy dog begging

for a branch of bleached wood, a man to throw it as far as he can.

Fantasy

The father parks outside the Pleasure Place
but does not turn off the ignition.
Tells his son, *I'll just be a second.* An hour later,
is found among the lifelike vaginas:
your mom wants something but I can't do it,
and when his kid asks, my father says, *rape*
fantasy, and his good son buys the video
while he sits in the car. *No big deal,*
I lie, handing over the paper bag
that means it's a sin to see inside.

*

The movie plays inside my head.
Every time I take to my bed alone,
begin the ritual, private tenderness,
I can't stop unreeling it, can't stop
the man, his chest above my face
so close I could punch him in his ribs,
scrape off skin or a nipple, anything
not to replay it exactly.

A Name I Could Not Say Aloud

One August night, a man will cook me dinner,
and rape me in his bed.

Before that, he'll play his piano
shirtless in the living room.

I will light the long-stemmed candles.
Water will boil on the stove.

When we eat, our knees will brush
and glance away under the table.

I will wash the dishes while he showers.
In the bedroom, the windows

will not be curtained.
Nothing makes them wince.

All the lights on. His shoulders
tan-lined, lightly hairy. I'll watch

the photo on the nightstand,
sepia rodeo man, lasso in hand,

I will think *cow-eyed* as he smiles,
tipping a Stetson toward me,

the heel of a real hand cupping my chin,
his name almost harmless: Martin.

The Piano

Where is this going, I thought,
as he played me the recording
in his spartan apartment
that summer, our shirts off,
and later, in his bed as he lie
on top of me, his fingers
in my mouth curling
around my uneven row
of keys, making me into
something he'd played
once, long ago in an emptied
church—no, not emptied,
since what he struck was music,
the will to live.

Genre Theory

There are two kinds of stories: my enemy watches
as I throw his dog over a cliff,
or some groundswell of mercy intervenes.

Two kinds of men: rapists and rapists-in-wait.

Two kinds of endings: tearful forgiveness and revenge arc.
My friend Michael invited me for Korean, unaware
of the restaurant's proximity to the apartment where
I was made an angry kind of story.

I imagine my rapist at home watching soaps
in his underwear, tan legs crossed on an ottoman,
his dog snoring beside him on the couch.
Imagining his legs doesn't help but the dog does.

I order water while I wait. Drink, checking the door
with a start every time a man enters. It's true,
no one can star in the story about his own degradation.

Every story is a tragedy infected by time.

Later, walking to the subway, I pass deliberately the place.
It's so dark out. It must be comedy unzipping.
I am so grateful for the water I drank, now a star-stream
of asparagus-piss at the brick of his building, urinating

in looping letters, as if I am writing the script
of his demise, a vinegar to fill his nostrils.

I swear I can hear the dog barking down at me,
barking for escape, barking out of love for me,
who had only ever dreamed him harmed.
But this is starting to turn into another kind of story
so I hurry away down into the subway, where the rats are,

down where Marilyn was always Norma Jeane,
where grit diamond-sparkles in rough light,
down where the understory waits its turn to be born,
invented by fairies, told around a fire, made up
by survivors, by the likes of you, and me.

Searching for Metaphor

My dead student demanded, *Look*,
standing outside my window, its curtain

thinner in the dawn. It was his voice
I woke to, the day of his funeral.

I put on my best shirt, I drove to the place
he was born. In the dream, I'd asked

for meaning, not direction, and so every
noun and gesture took on the patina

of loss: the ambulance on the highway,
its driver flipping me off for going too slow,

and in the parking lot the buzzards huddled
around a struck fox, unfoxing it, the torn

intestines' primal dark—or during the service,
the pastor saying his name and the door

opening suddenly, light bounding in.
In the coffin, he did not seem asleep.

Silk lining, silk cushion, dead boy, *Look!*,
refusing to be transformed.

Out from the Patches
of Briers and Blackberries

After he died, my father made whole
again, he kept close to my mother
as she smoked on the couch,
his face more alive than at Christmas,
the last time I saw him, struggling
to lift his cup. He could show off
an even row of teeth, now, wry
and silly, to score some irony
in the situation, but the days I was home,
he didn't smile. My mother was in pain,
he was the source, he grieved with her.
And though he died on the same day
as my father, my student waited a week
to visit. In the dream, his back was all
he'd allow, the sweep of curls: another boy
Apollo. He was shy about his neck.
I asked him to show me where he'd been
hurt, his purpled throat. He couldn't
breathe a word, but I saw in him
a glimmer. Our dead return,
wanting us to know there is no end.

Even suffering outlives this body.

Musical

Her mouth kept open by breathing duct,
chest rhythmic under the starched sheet.

A skin scoured clean as a polished floor
in an emptied house, for sale. Gone, the garden

grit underneath her fingernails. It's not her,
I thought, watching her heart take forty minutes

to stop. At the funeral, not a flower in sight,
the dark purple smell of her ungloved hands

crossed over to me, and I could see her
pruning the plum tree, gritting her teeth,

planting the geraniums out back. But she was
dead, and we were at the cemetery,

burying my grandmother alive.

*

My grandmother loved *The Music Man*, *Pete's Dragon*
—peppy anthems leading the parade all the way

to the town's square. Loved snare drums, hurrying banjos,
trumpeters—exit music. But her death was six shades

of quiet. My grandmother's singing voice might have been
smoky, opulent countertenor, breaking like it did

the time she told me she loved me.
Now the machines sing for her, sharp notes

that mean one cranial hemisphere, the musical one,
is shoving against the other. She loved music

but I never heard her sing. She was afraid
of her voice betraying sentiment. I will sing now

I am no longer afraid to die.

Please Enjoy These Coming Attractions

A friend keeps writing about the little blue pills,
every poem a time bomb he plants inside his body.

My little brother says he knows how he'll end it too:
plastic bag over his head, cinched with rubber bands.

A lover said he loaded the gun once, clicked the safety
off, held it to his head. The barrel left a surprised O

at his temple for a day. My former teacher crushes crystals,
dirty gray, in a bowl, then holds them in his palm,

the charred remains of pleasure. The college freshman
shows me the delicate x's the X-Acto made, crossing

his blue veins at sixteen. Chris hanged himself
on a closet door with hotel towels on vacation in Peru.

Every gay man inhabiting my students' short stories
crossed out by AIDS or hate crime. Is it any wonder

I have failed to imagine my life won't end
in autopsy? Hey, straight reader.

Spin this loaded gun between us.
Let's see whose life it chooses.

Early English History

Was too early: 8 a.m. Tuesday/Thursday, Elizabeth Hall.
I slouched half-asleep, first-rowed, demarcated
from the frat boys sitting in back so they could see
up the professor's skirt. In the mead hall after,
they surrounded, let me close if I shared my notes.
I was in love with the black-haired outfielder,
his backwards Braves cap, until he called me *fag*
for refusing to rate our teacher's underwear.
I didn't know how to fight back. I learned that semester
about the rebel queen Boudica, whose revolt razed
three Roman forts and the emperor's temple.
Tacitus provides motive: her husband dead, kingdom
annexed, Boudica flogged, her daughters raped.
The armies she led tortured its captives
but he doesn't say why. Some pain is negligible;
its survival cancels the wound of its birth.
Most accounts say she poisoned herself,
facing defeat. Cassius Dio gives her longer:
secreted away to the south, living unrecorded
for years with her daughters. The boys in my class
drew stick figures fucking on the wall by my room
after I came out. I woke at night to wash out
the crooked glyphs, the caption proclaiming
"AIDES kills faggs dead." I scrubbed until
what remained was fist-sized, vague and pink,
a map of the possible world. Our final project
was to cook an authentic English banquet,

eaten family-style at the professor's house.
At the appointed time in the year of our lord,
I came with dessert but did not see the moat
she'd installed in her foyer. The strawberry pudding
flew like an arrow, pink spurting everywhere,
especially across the faces of those boys whose names
were lost the moment I joined an insurrection
begun in AD 61 by a dissident queen. In the years
since my disappearance, I have cemented
my escarpments, foddered my canon, sewn up
my flag. I am painting my face, bluing my body
with woad. Warn them. I am coming
to punish my Romans.

Boy with the Head of Goliath

The boy facing the light in Caravaggio's painting—
after he finishes his good work, David
raises Goliath's head; the body missing.

When I was David, I couldn't fight like that.
I could only pray to be changed. It took years,
but the angel came, outlined my neck with his teeth.
We slept, he fit me to his chest, he choked me awake.

If I could only tell that boy, *It's almost done, I know
it hurts, I'm sorry.* But even this close he can't hear.
For him, nothing will add up again.

He'll be bad at math, bad at defining the limits
of x as it approaches infinity;

bad at history, confusing the names of barbaric kings.
Every man is a rapist.

It's so hard to face the light, to square your body
to the oncoming plot, hard to survive
everything yet to be imagined. There's no one left
who remembers who I was.

And yet: I am holding up my head. I am
doing my work. I am alive,
if only out of vengeance.

Romantic Comedy

Enchanted (2007)

Goddamn the snow that sent me into the theater
for two hours' refuge in projected light. Even if
I only wanted escape, goddamn my wanting.
Goddamn the romantic comedy, a genre pockmarked
by selves who never fulfill themselves. Goddamn
the men like me, holding hands next to me in the dark,
their snippets of growl gilding the film, their delight
at the comic heroine's transformation from cartoon
to flesh. She falls from Technicolor to Times Square,
rising from the underground in her marriage gown.
Goddamn her flawless skin, her eyes rinsed red,
waking in a drainpipe at the beginning of a soured century.
And then, God, after the movie's over and I've been flung
into another city's sprawl, after I've been released
from the fold forlorn, damn the bride emerging
from the Renaissance Hotel across the salted avenue,
a vision in an unsullied dress. Goddamn the fabric
so luminous in the portrait, looming from its frame,
filling us with longing to bite it into shreds. Goddamn,
what's wrong with me? I can't stop thinking about the fairytale
princess, her optimism a perfumed wind in a flagging sail.
As if no one is shipwrecked on the shores of Love
Always Fails Us. The groom is whispering, *Goddamn*
you're wet in the hotel laundry to a bridesmaid
whose white fur wrap is a strip of fallen weather
on the cement floor. Goddamn all beauty made in betrayal.

Goddamn the bride, she wants to live the heroine's life,
all shivering lip and beaded veil, goddamn her
until she is weeping, the cartoon fool. The goddamn concierge
opens the car door for her, bending elegantly
at the waist to palm her dress into the limousine.
He fingers the slight hem. Goddamn him, showing us
what he could do to skin on the belly, skin on the thigh,
my untouched cheek. Goddamn the wind, it isn't the hand
of a lover. Goddamn the wineglass shattering inexplicably
at the best man's toast. The best men, the worst men, the extras
in the movie which brought me to tears—goddamn them
and the gift of my body. Goddamn the land and the air,
the fish and the fowl, the light in the day and the night
in the night. But do not damn the lit cigarette I'm holding
too close to my face. Not it, God. Though it burns acrid
between my fingers, it does not leave me alone to lift
my face up out of the halo of darkness, in the cold of Chicago.

Underground Premonition

We stay up all night, snorting Adderall
off each other's backs, drinking bourbon,
until I confuse time and story, thinking
one is harnessed to the other,

until I am looking down at faint pink lines
above his ass and suddenly he's all of them
—Zürich suicide, my beautiful Madrileño,
the swim coach, the rapist pianist—the men
I could not save, dissolving into periphery.

It's New York, tomorrow. We're two men
in cargo shorts in a station: the subway
at 191 Street. He takes a paper
for the crossword, we wait in the dark,
two opposite-facing parentheses.

It doesn't sadden me now
I see how the story ends.

NOTES

"Lie Down Where Their Faces Are": The title comes from Anne
Sexton's poem, "A Curse Against Elegies" in which the speaker
says, "lie down where you think their faces are; / talk back to
your old bad dreams."

"Night Watch": Allen Ginsberg's poem "Please Master" mixes
erotic, pornographic, and Romantic diction.

"Erotic Crime Thriller": William Friedkin wrote and directed
Cruising, starring Al Pacino as a cop who goes undercover
to catch a serial killer preying on men in the queer leather/
levi and BDSM communities. The killer seems to jump bodies
(he seems to be played by different actors throughout the
film)—implying that, by the end, it may be Pacino's character,
as he stares into the camera-via-bathroom-mirror while
his girlfriend tries on the leather jacket, cap, and aviator
sunglasses we see the killer wear throughout the film.

"The Saw": During the Spanish Inquisition, the saw became
a popular torture device, since traveling inquisitors could
borrow it from local villagers. Inverting the prisoner meant
that blood diverted to the brain, minimizing gore. While
some victims apparently were severed completely in half,
most were only sawed to the abdomen. This prolonged the
suffering and time until death. And, for sodomites (later
called "inverts"), it gestured symbolically to the areas that
offended God.

"Stock Character": The notion of "types" in drama owes itself to
commedia dell'arte, a kind of improvisational street theater
that used archetypes which were obvious to the audience.

Commedia dell'arte gives us the grammar for many genres and is an early precursor to the romantic comedy.

"The Bridge": James Baldwin published *Another Country* in 1962. Rufus is a jazz drummer who kills himself after a dysfunctional love affair ends.

"One Train's Survival Depends on the Other Derailed": Susan Mitchell's poem "A Story" (from *Rapture*) begins "There is a bar I go to when I'm in Chicago / which is like a bar I used to go to when I lived in New York."

"Monument": George C. Boldt, millionaire proprietor of the Waldorf-Astoria Hotel in New York City, purchased Hart Island at the turn of the 20th century. After changing both its name and its shape to resemble a more conventional valentine, he then started construction on a full-size Rhineland castle on its land. This grand gesture was a display of love for his wife, who died in 1904 as the castle neared finishing. Boldt telegraphed to stop construction, and the house lay unfinished until 1977, when it was acquired by the Thousand Islands Bridge Authority for $1.00.

Adam Walsh was abducted from a mall in Hollywood, Florida on July 27, 1981. Two fishermen in Vero Beach found his severed head on August 10. Three weeks later, I started first grade.

"Genre Theory": Peter (Stephen Fry) in *Peter's Friends* doesn't technically die, but he reveals he is HIV-positive and the characters gather around him as if surrounding a death-bed.

"On Dark Days, I Imagine My Parents' Wedding Video": Anita Bryant, a former Miss Oklahoma who went on to be a spokesperson for Florida Orange Juice, helmed the *Save Our Children* campaign, which led to repealing anti-discrimination laws in Miami-Dade County. She took her homophobic show on the road, and on October 14, 1978 she was met with a protestor who pied her in the face at a press conference. Little is known about the protestor, Thom L. Higgins, who died in his mid-forties in 1994, most likely due to complications from AIDS.

"Hart Crane Aboard the Steamship Orizaba": Hart Crane jumped off the *Orizaba* into the Gulf of Mexico just before noon on April 27, 1932. *Orizaba* means "valley of happy waters."

"Out from the Patches of Briers and Blackberries": The title is verbatim a line from Whitman's "Out of the Cradle Endlessly Rocking." The poem remembers both my father and a former student who died the same day.

"Early English History": Boudica led the Celtic Iceni in a revolt against the Romans in East Anglia in AD 60 or 61.

"Boy with the Head of Goliath": Caravaggio painted David severing Goliath's head at least three separate times, always using his own face as that of the monster. The painting mentioned here is exhibited in the Prado Museum in Madrid, Spain.

"Romantic Comedy": The film *Enchanted* is a 2007 American romantic comedy starring Amy Adams as a Disney princess who falls from cartoon reality into the live-action world of New York City.

THANKS

I am endlessly grateful to Jericho Brown, Mark Doty, Jehanne Dubrow, Michael Dumanis, Lindsay Lusby, and Aaron Smith for their friendship and guidance. A special thanks goes to Miguel Murphy who helped to re-envision and refine this book. I'm indebted to Washington College for a junior sabbatical leave, as well as to the University of Arizona Poetry Center Fieries and Snuffies Summer Residency Program, the Bread Loaf Writers' Conference, and the Sewanee Writers' Conference. Thanks go also to Diane Seuss for choosing this book and to the team at Four Way Books for everything they've done to turn it into a reality. To my brothers, Dustin and C.J. Hall, thank you for your corroborations and questions.

I am daily grateful for Anthony Raley—the best leading man a guy could ask for.

ACKNOWLEDGMENTS

I am grateful to the editors of the following literary journals in which these poems appeared, sometimes in different versions:

A&U: America's AIDS Magazine, Academy of American Poets *Poem-a-Day, Agni, American Poetry Review, Arts & Letters, Bloom, Cimarron Review, Connotation Press, Cortland Review, Diagram, Diode, Fledgling Rag, Four Way Review, Fourteen Hills, The Georgia Review, The Journal, JuxtaProse, New England Review, Ninth Letter, Notre Dame Review, Pembroke Magazine, Phantom Limb, Pittsburgh Poetry Review, Pleiades: Literature in Context, The Summerset Review, Twelfth House,* and *Vinyl Poetry.*

"One Train's Survival Depends on the Other Derailed" also appeared in *Best American Poetry 2012,* edited by Mark Doty and David Lehman. "Not Her Body" appeared in *The Book of Scented Things,* edited by Jehanne Dubrow and Lindsay Lusby.

JAMES ALLEN HALL (he/they) is the author of a previous book of poems, *Now You're the Enemy*, and *I Liked You Better Before I Knew You So Well*, a book of lyric essays. They direct the Rose O'Neill Literary House at Washington College.

PUBLICATION OF THIS BOOK WAS MADE POSSIBLE BY GRANTS AND DONATIONS. WE ARE ALSO GRATEFUL TO THOSE INDIVIDUALS WHO PARTICIPATED IN OUR 2022 BUILD A BOOK PROGRAM. THEY ARE:

Anonymous (12), Robert Abrams, Michael Ansara, Kathy Aponick, Jean Ball, Sally Ball, Clayre Benzadón, Adrian Blevins, Laurel Blossom, adam bohannon, Betsy Bonner, Patricia Bottomley, Lee Briccetti, Joel Brouwer, Susan Buttenwieser, Anthony Cappo, Paul and Brandy Carlson, Mark Conway, Elinor Cramer, Dan and Karen Clarke, Kwame Dawes, Michael Anna de Armas, John Del Peschio, Brian Komei Dempster, Rosalynde Vas Dias, Patrick Donnelly, Lynn Emanuel, Blas Falconer, Jennifer Franklin, John Gallaher, Reginald Gibbons, Rebecca Kaiser Gibson, Dorothy Tapper Goldman, Julia Guez, Naomi Guttman and Jonathan Mead, Forrest Hamer, Luke Hankins, Yona Harvey, KT Herr, Karen Hildebrand, Carlie Hoffman, Glenna Horton, Thomas and Autumn Howard, Catherine Hoyser, Elizabeth Jackson, Linda Susan Jackson, Jessica Jacobs and Nickole Brown, Lee Jenkins, Elizabeth Kanell, Nancy Kassell, Maeve Kinkead, Victoria Korth, Brett Lauer and Gretchen Scott, Howard Levy, Owen Lewis and Susan Ennis, Margaree Little, Sara London and Dean Albarelli, Tariq Luthun, Myra Malkin, Louise Mathias, Victoria McCoy, Lupe Mendez, Michael and Nancy Murphy, Kimberly Nunes, Susan Okie and Walter Weiss, Cathy McArthur Palermo, Veronica Patterson, Jill Pearlman, Marcia and Chris Pelletiere, Sam Perkins, Susan Peters and Morgan Driscoll, Maya Pindyck, Megan Pinto, Kevin Prufer, Martha Rhodes, Paula Rhodes, Louise Riemer, Peter and Jill Schireson, Rob Schlegel, Yoana Setzer, Soraya Shalforoosh, Mary Slechta, Diane Souvaine, Barbara Spark, Catherine Stearns, Jacob Strautmann, Yerra Sugarman, Arthur Sze and Carol Moldaw, Marjorie and Lew Tesser, Dorothy Thomas, Rushi Vyas, Martha Webster and Robert Fuentes, Rachel Weintraub and Allston James, Jane and Jonathan Wells, Abigail Wender, D. Wolff, Monica Youn